Tokay
Gecko
Care

Quick & Easy Tokay Gecko Care

Project Team
Editor: Brian Scott
Copy Editor: Stephanie Hays
Design: Patricia Escabi
Series Design: Mary Ann Kahn

T.F.H. Publications
President/CEO: Glen S. Axelrod
Executive Vice President: Mark E. Johnson
Publisher: Christopher T. Reggio
Production Manager: Kathy Bontz

T.F.H. Publications, Inc.
One TFH Plaza
Third and Union Avenues
Neptune City, NJ 07753

05 06 07 08 09 1 3 5 7 9 8 6 4 2

Library of Congress Cataloging-in-Publication Data
Both, Allen
Quick and easy tokay gecko care / Allen Both
p. cm.
Includes index.
ISBN 0-7938-1017-5 (alk. paper)
1. Tokay geckos as pets. I. Title.
SF459.G35B68 2005
597.9'52--dc22
2005007797

The Leader In Responsible Animal Care For Over 50 Years! ™
www.tfhpublications.com

Table
of Contents

Introduction: What Are Geckos?

In recent years, the general public has become very aware of geckos. From television advertisements to print ads, the term *gecko* is easily recognized by nearly everyone in today's society. With entire channels on television dedicated to animals, these interesting lizards are constantly in the spotlight, and such a high level of exposure leads many people to seek out these animals as pets.

Geckos are a highly diversified group of lizards comprised of about 300 species worldwide. Some of them are terrestrial (ground-dwellers), while others are arboreal (tree-dwellers). Some make vocal sounds, while others don't make a sound at all. Some

Geckos are a highly diversified group of lizards comprised of about 300 species worldwide.

have stunning colors and patterns, while others are drab and basically colorless. With so many species to choose from which to choose and with such an interesting array of attributes, it is easy to see how geckos have become so recognized in our society.

This book will focus on just one species within this amazingly interesting group of lizards—the tokay gecko. In it, you will find basic but very useful information on the following subjects: natural history, housing, diet and nutrition, reproduction, and a host of other informational tidbits that will help you keep your tokay geckos happy and healthy for years.

Introducing the Tokay Gecko

Tokay geckos are famous for the unique vocalizations they make. This loud call sounds like the lizard is saying *toe-kay*, *toe-kay*, which is where their common name originated, and can carry quite a distance. The males make these calls to stake out territory, and although females will sometimes vocalize, too, it is much less common. Both sexes will make a loud clicking/growling noise when they feel threatened and are about to bite—something to be cautious of as their bites sometimes require stitches!

Natural Range & Habitat

Tokay geckos naturally inhabit Japan, China, Indonesia, and much of southern Asia and are often imported for the pet trade from

Tokay geckos make loud vocalizations. These loud calls sound like the gecko is saying "toe-kay, toe-kay," which is where their common name originated.

Vietnam. However, they can also be found in many parts of the world where they are not native. This is believed to be a direct result of the geckos becoming stowaways on plants and in cargo being shipped around the world. In fact, the United States even has populations of these animals in parts of Florida. These populations may be results of large numbers being imported for the pet trade and finding their way to freedom by one manner or another. One major problem has been the purchase and release of these animals as a method of "natural" pest control to mainly consume cockroaches and the like.

Tokay geckos come from open forest areas and are very tolerant of human civilization. They are often found on the walls of buildings in many cities throughout southern Asia. Cities and towns have plenty of outdoor areas lit by artificial lights, and these places are

Eyes of the Cat

Species of nocturnal geckos (i.e., the tokay gecko included) generally have a vertical pupil. This type of pupil seems to give them better vision in the dark for hunting and exploring, as it is more selective about the amount of light that's allowed to pass into the eye.

virtual food dispensers for tokay geckos in the night. Roaches, moths, and a vast array of other tropical insects flock to the light source when the sun goes down—just in time for these nocturnal creatures to begin their day.

Physical description

Tokay geckos are one of the largest geckos in the world, sometimes reaching in excess of 10 inches (25 cm) in total length (TL). They have long, thin tails, which will break if handled roughly. They have large feet with wide, rounded pads, which allow them to climb on almost any surface. They also have a robust head with extremely strong jaw muscles. Their eyes are bright gold with vertical pupils.

Handling Your Tokay Gecko

Some people suggest wearing a pair of heavy gloves when first attempting to tame a tokay. If you are starting out with a baby, the bite won't be bad and the gloves may not be necessary. Baby tokay geckos will be a better choice to start with if you are set on having a pet you can handle, although if you want a truly tame lizard, you are better purchasing a bearded dragon or spiny-tailed agama.

Be careful when handling tokays so you do not rip their skin. They have pretty tough skin, but if handled too roughly, the skin can become damaged. Damaged skin can open up the possibility of infection, which can lead to the demise of your pet.

If you apply too much pressure to the tail, it will break and the gecko will likely get away. The tails will regrow but will never have the same look as the original tail.

The thing to remember with attempting to tame your tokay gecko is patience and persistence. The more time you work with them and the less you get discouraged, the more likely it is that your gecko will be able to be handled.

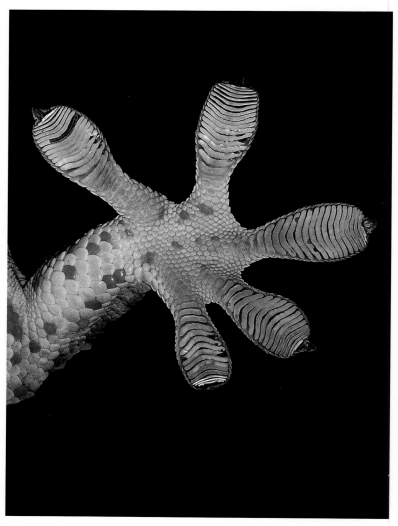

Tokay geckos have large feet with wide, rounded pads, which allow them to climb on nearly any surface.

Quick & Easy Tokay Gecko Care

Rows of large red spots occur in a uniform fashion along the back of tokay geckos. These spots make the lizards appear quite colorful.

Babies are darker in color than the adults and have seven to ten rows of round white spots. They also have white-banded tails, making the babies very attractive to prospective hobbyists wishing to add a tokay gecko to their collection. Red spots occur on the back in rather uniform rows and make the animal, in some instances, quite colorful. As the gecko matures, the darker skin color tends to become grayer or light pastel blue in color, the white spots tend to fade, and the red spots change to orange and become more evident. Well-conditioned adults are some of the most colorful lizards you can buy.

Captive-Bred Specimens

Many people do not have the time to devote to a strict handling schedule, and paying a little extra for a captive-bred and already tame specimen may be the right road to travel. Make sure you locate a reputable breeder who stands behind his or her product if you are looking for such a lizard, and don't be afraid to spend some extra money. Sometimes it's true—you do get what you pay for.

No Eyelids

Tokay geckos are members of the family Gekkonidae and are considered "true" geckos. These geckos have no moveable eyelids but rather a single scale called a spectacle or brille that covers their eyes. This serves as a protective cover. Tokay geckos will remove droplets of water or any dirt from their eyes by licking them, an adaptation that is very interesting and common with geckos in this family.

Behavioral Characteristics

Tokay geckos are not necessarily the right pet for everyone and have for many years been regarded as a highly aggressive terrarium animal that should not be handled. In recent years, a few reptile breeders have noticed some good pet potential for this species based solely on their size and color. Through captive-breeding programs and regular handling of them while young, some tokay geckos can become rather tame.

With their large and powerful mouths, tokays have been know to bite their keepers—sometimes quite badly.

Quick & Easy Tokay Gecko Care

Some folks refer to anoles as "geckos." However, they are a completely unrelated group of lizards, although many require the same care as tokay geckos.

Introducing the Tokay Gecko

Tokay geckos vary a lot in their coloration and pattern. Note the nicely patterned head of this specimen.

If you're interested in having a large gecko that you can handle, you must remember that not all that are offered for sale are tame and captive bred. It will require a lot of work and a lot of patience to get them to the point where they will be content to just sit on your shoulder, and you must realize that not all tokay geckos are even capable of becoming so tame.

Color Morphs

As with many other species of reptiles that are being captive bred, different color morphs sometimes pop up after years of captive breeding. Sometimes genetic oddities are even found in the wild, brought to captivity, and cultivated into a new designer lizard or snake. At the time of this writing, tokay geckos are no exception. Albino, leucistic (white and yellow) and even a piebald (normal color with patches of pure white) genetic abnormality have been discovered, and breeders are trying to cultivate these morphs into something that will be readily available down the road.

Considerations Before Purchasing

When deciding on the purchase of a tokay gecko, be sure to take several things into consideration. Of course, you'll want to select a healthy specimen. Make sure the body weight is good; a healthy tokay gecko will not have hip bones showing or sunken eyes. The color should be normal, and specimens that appear very dark are usually stressed. If not housed under the proper conditions, they may perish and probably should be avoided entirely.

Of course, when considering the purchase of any reptile, you *must* do your research on that particular animal. Become familiar with the requirements that must be met to successfully care for your new lizard. Reading books such as this one and carefully examining what types of caging are suitable is another important step in preparing yourself properly. After learning the basics of what is required, be sure to set up the environment ahead of time. It is always better to be prepared so there is minimal time for the animal to be in transit and out of its proper environment.

The Big Day

Once you have selected your gecko, it is time to bring him home and place him in his new cage. You're going to need to allow the

Herp is the Word

Throughout this book, you will see the term *herps*. This word refers to both reptiles and amphibians together and comes from the word *herpetology*, which is the study of reptiles and amphibians. *Herpetoculture* is the keeping and breeding of reptiles and amphibians. A *herper* is someone who participates in the herp hobby or herpetoculture (also called a *herp hobbyist*).

These terms are handy to know, not just for reading this book, but because you will see them in other herp publications and on the Internet, and you will hear other hobbyists use them.

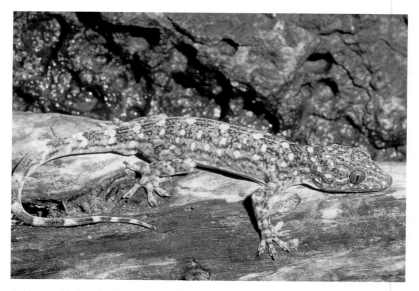

This marbled gecko has very similar care and husbandry requirements as a tokay gecko.

gecko to acclimate to his new surroundings for a little while before attempting to pick him up or even feed him. The best way to do this is by simply sitting back and observing him for a few days. After a full 24-hour period, you can offer him some food, usually in the form of small living insects. Of course, be sure that there is ample fresh water that's able to be accessed at any time, because the gecko may need to rehydrate himself after the transition from one place to another. If you follow these simple guidelines, you are well on your way to keeping your new pet.

Quick & Easy Tokay Gecko Care

Housing Your Tokay Gecko

When choosing the cage in which your gecko will be housed, there are a few things you will need to know. The overall space and dimensions of a cage that would be required for an arboreal species (like the tokay gecko) may be quite different from those of a terrestrial species (like the leopard gecko).

For tokay geckos, it's important to provide a cage that is as at least as tall as it is long. For example, if your cage is 24 inches (60 cm) long, then it should be at least 24 inches (60 cm) tall (or even a bit taller). Because the most common type of caging available are glass aquariums, one or two adult tokay geckos would probably have little difficulty being housed in a 20-gallon (76 l) "extra-high" tank, which measures 20" (50 cm) long by 24" (60 cm) tall.

Using Glass Aquariums

If using a glass aquarium, you will also need to get a sturdy screen cover. Most pet stores sell screen lids to fit the aquariums they sell. Of course, if you choose an aquarium that is a custom or nonstandard size, you may need to have a screen lid specially made for you. Make sure to also get cage clips or another locking device. These will help to lock the cage shut so your geckos do not push their way to freedom.

Until now, we have been referring to aquariums in their normal way of sitting, which is upright with the opening on the top. For arboreal geckos such as tokays, you can also use an aquarium in an alternate fashion. The method for making an "extra-tall" type enclosure for arboreal lizards requires taking a 20- or 30-gallon (76 to114 l) long aquarium and standing it on end with the opening of the cage facing out or to the side (your preference). While this

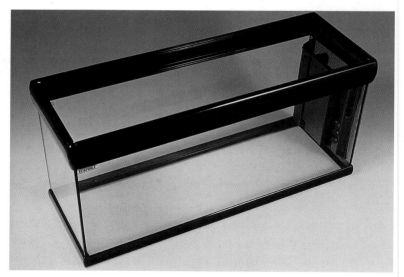

Glass aquariums are the most common type of housing for all types of geckos— tokays included.

It's not uncommon to find geckos hanging out in the strangest of positions. This gold gecko decided that he wanted to hang upside down while waiting for a meal to pass by.

Housing Your Tokay Gecko

arrangement provides a lot of useful space for your gecko, it can present a problem when trying to contain the animal from escaping the large opening, and it also leaves you with no way of holding your substrate in the cage.

To remedy this, you will need a piece of Plexiglas or glass cut to the size of the opening so that it will rest right in the rim of the tank. Make this piece of glass is one-third to one-half of the opening size. This will help you solve the dilemma of containing the substrate and having too large of an opening for the animal to escape. Use aquarium sealant to make the new partial front a bit more permanent and hold the glass or Plexiglas in place. You will also need to add a screen door so you can access the water bowl, clean the cage, and get the gecko out when you need to. The door can be made of screen and fitted with plastic hinges, or you can simply use a regular aquarium screen cover with the same clips mentioned earlier.

If retrofitting a custom terrarium for your gecko seems like too much work, commercial cages for arboreal herps are available for sale. There are cages made of PVC, glass, plastic, and wood that are offered through pet retailers and cage manufacturers, and they are becoming increasingly more common as reptiles become more and more popular as pets. Some of these cages are quite attractive, and if you are looking for something suitable for a certain room in your house, the odds are good that you will find it.

Choosing a Substrate

Once a cage has been chosen, you will need to outfit it. For starters, you will need substrate. You may often hear terms such as *litter* or *bedding*, but these are all synonymous terms used for the cover that will line the bottom of the cage. For tokay geckos, a substrate that holds a bit of humidity is best, like red cypress mulch, for example.

Other substrates that should work well in a tokay gecko's cage are orchid bark, recycled paper bedding, potting soil, and various

There are many types of substrates that can be used for lining the bottom of your tokay's cage. Be sure to ask your dealer for recommendations.

other types of substrates that are marketed for use in terrariums. Potting soil is usually reserved for use in elaborate setups where live plants are going to be employed in the landscape design of the enclosure. Gravel or vermiculite can also be used, but gravel tends to be more difficult to keep clean because it is not absorbent, and vermiculite tends to be very messy to work with. Additionally, gravel poses a risk of causing a gut impaction in your gecko (a serious and life-threatening blockage of the digestive tract).

Regardless of the substrate you select, the entire cage bottom should be covered to a depth of about 1 inch (2.5 cm). If you're using potting soil in a cage with live plants, you should also include about 1 inch (2.5 cm) of pea gravel beneath the soil. This will serve as a drainage layer and will prevent the soil from becoming soggy. Soil that remains too damp will harbor mites and bacteria, both of which can cause harm to your tokay gecko.

Cage Furniture and Decorations

When choosing how to decorate your cage, you can keep it simple or make it elaborate. With tokay geckos, either simple or elaborate

Using Potting Soil

Many potting soils contain a material called perlite, which is a granular white material of mineral origin. Others contain little particles of Styrofoam. These materials are added to increase drainage and aeration of the soil. While these materials are good for plants, they can cause problems for your lizards. Both perlite and Styrofoam can cause gut impactions, which can be fatal to your tokay gecko. It's best to buy potting soils that do not contain these materials. Unfortunately, most potting soils contain one or the other, but organic potting soils should contain neither. Therefore, it is best to use organic potting soils for substrates and in the pots of any plants you place in your lizard's enclosure.

types of setups will be suitable as long as the decorations are as well. Let's start with a simple approach.

The Simple Approach

Furnish the cage with one of the types of substrates that discussed earlier. There are many options when it comes to adding cage furnishings. For arboreal geckos, such as tokay geckos, it is good to provide something for them to climb on. Driftwood, cork bark, or

A simple approach is to use a few large rocks, perhaps a couple pieces of wood, and an easy-to-clean substrate.

grape wood is all readily available commercial cage furnishings that will suit your lizard nicely. Cork backing often comes in a tube or semi-cylindrical shape, giving your gecko a nice, snug hiding place that he is sure to frequent. Polyresin replicas are also popular; they look natural and are easy to clean, unlike the real thing. These types of décor can be found in most pet stores.

Artificial plants can be added to provide some cover, giving the tokay gecko a sense of security during daylight hours. They also add to the aesthetics of the enclosure. Different types of fake plants are readily available, and there is no shortage of life-like decorations to really enhance the look of your enclosure. Many hobbyists prefer the ones that stick to the sides of a glass enclosure with suction cups. These can be used to create a nice backdrop in the terrarium.

Naturalistic Vivarium

If you are interested in creating a more elaborate and natural setup, you can design what's known as a "naturalistic vivarium." These types of enclosures are commonplace in the European herp hobby, and they seem to be gaining popularity in the United States. They can be quite eye-catching works of art rather than just simple reptile caging. Best of all, the act of setting up a naturalistic vivarium can be a fun and educational project in which the whole family can participate.

Naturalistic vivariums are more elaborate and require additional time and resources in order to maintain them properly.

Some naturalistic vivariums have multiple tiers for the lizards to inhabit. Such displays are usually very beautiful as long as they are maintained properly.

Just as with the simple approach, you'll need to provide a substrate first. Naturalistic vivariums need a bi-level substrate base in order to provide the proper environment for the roots of live plants to grow and flourish. Start with a gravel or vermiculite bottom layer, as either one will assist in drainage of the top layer (soil). Potting soil or peat moss can be used for a top layer that is ideal for planting live plants. There are many different types of potting soils available, so make sure to read the package thoroughly. Always avoid soil that contains insecticides and fungicides; these chemicals can harm your animals. African violet potting soil is very rich and works well for most of the plants you can keep in this type of enclosure.

Once your substrate is in place, you can begin to furnish the vivarium. For tokay geckos, which are generally found in wide-open forests, branches or cork bark make the best climbing furniture. Cork bark can even be fixed to the sides of the cage with aquarium sealant for a more permanent display. However, this can lead to problems keeping the cage clean. You will have to be extra diligent in this regard. Sturdy pieces of driftwood can also be added to decorate the sides and back of the cage. With so many different types of decorations available from pet retailers and reptile suppliers today, the possibilities of creating an enchanting environment are nearly endless. The cage can be as complicated or as simple as you want to make it, but be aware

Quick & Easy Tokay Gecko Care

that the more complicated you make it, the more work it may take to maintain it.

When selecting plants to furnish the cage, you again have a wealth of possibilities at your fingertips. Always take into consideration the requirements of the plants, as well as the animals, in this type of enclosure. For tokay geckos, choose plants that do not have high lighting requirements. Tokay geckos are nocturnal, and long hours of lighting that live plants often need may not be good for your gecko. To offset this, make sure your geckos have plenty of hiding places so they can stay out of the light when they want to—which will be most of the time.

Because tokay geckos are a large species of gecko, they may become somewhat destructive to delicate plants while moving around the enclosure. Be sure to select hardier, sturdier broad-leafed plants that will not be easily disturbed by the gecko. When positioning the plants, try to keep most of them toward the back of the enclosure. The gecko will likely try to hide around the plants, giving him less

While tokays certainly appreciate the cover that plants provide, they may damage delicate species due to the lizard's weight. Be sure to choose sturdy plants for your terrarium.

Housing Your Tokay Gecko

Water bowls should be thoroughly cleaned on a regular basis.

chance to defecate on the front glass, which will keep your cage looking clean. Lastly, be sure to rinse the plant's leaves and roots thoroughly before inserting them into the cage. This will wash off any residual insecticides that may be on the plant itself.

After the soil is washed off, you can either set the plants right in the substrate of the vivarium, or you can pot them individually. If using pots, sink the pots down into the substrate or hide them behind cage furnishings to prevent them from spoiling the natural look you are trying to achieve.

Water and Humidity

Tokay geckos don't really need high humidity in their enclosure. In fact, humidity levels of 50 to 75 percent are usually adequate for adult animals. Juveniles seem to prefer slightly higher humidity, which probably has to do with the microhabitats (like tree trunks) that the hatchlings initially choose to live in after hatching out from their eggs. When acquiring a new wild-caught specimen, try to maintain the humidity on the higher side until the animal is acclimated and well hydrated in his new environment. Having a hygrometer (a device that measures the humidity in the air) is a good idea.

Water Bowls

A water bowl should be provided and always filled with clean water for drinking. It is also a good practice to mist the cage once or twice

Reptiles Are Not Cold-Blooded

Although you may have been taught to think of reptiles as cold-blooded animals, this is now known to be an inaccurate description. Scientists believe reptiles are not necessarily cold-blooded; rather, they are pokilothermic. A pokilothermic animal takes on the temperature of its outside environment, thus changing the temperature of its blood. This is a reason thermoregulation is so important to captive reptiles. Reptiles use their behavior to maintain temperatures in their preferred range. Some reptiles actually maintain body temperatures higher than many mammals. Because reptiles use the environment to provide their heat, they use less food energy to heat themselves than mammals and birds and can survive and thrive with much less food. Rather than thinking of this as a primitive or inferior system, think of it as just another way to accomplish the task of heating the body.

daily. Tokays will drink from the bowl as well as lap droplets of water that collect on the glass, plants, and decorations. Be sure to change the water daily and wipe the bowl clean to reduce harmful bacteria levels. Tokay geckos are an arboreal species, so an elevated water bowl is not a bad idea. Some naturalistic vivariums can have bowls positioned up in the branches to provide a more easily accessible water source.

Water bowls are available in many shapes, sizes, and styles. Choose a water bowl that is at least 4 inches in diameter and about 1 inch deep. When selecting a water bowl, there are several options for today's reptile keeper. Simple round ceramic bowls will be sufficient, but if you are looking for something more attractive, pet retailers now offer naturalistic stone and resin water bowls.

Heating and Lighting

Unlike many other lizards, tokay geckos do not have a need for

ultraviolet lighting. Being a nocturnal species (active by night), tokay geckos do not benefit from full-spectrum lighting like a diurnal animal (active by day) would require. In naturalistic vivariums, a few hours of full-spectrum lighting on a daily basis are necessary for the plants to flourish, although it should not be prolonged because the gecko doesn't require it.

Most geckos don't have a need for ultraviolet lighting since they are primarily nocturnal lizards.

Heat Lamps

A heat lamp is the only necessary lighting for tokay geckos. Temperatures of 78° to 86°F during the day are best with a 10 to 15 degree temperature drop at night—something easily achieved by using heat lamps.

Heat lamps get very hot and may burn your lizard if they get too close to them. Always make sure that there is a screen between the animal and the lights.

For example, on a 20-gallon (76 l) high terrarium at normal room temperature (~65°F/18.3C), you will most likely need a 100 to 150 watt heat bulb to create the 78° to 86°F (25.5 to 30C) temperature. Provide this heat for eight to ten hours a day during normal daylight times. Later, switching to either a 75 or 100 watt red-colored bulb or a nightlight-type bulb during dark hours will give you the nighttime temperature drop needed. These bulbs are commonly found in most pet retailers that carry reptile supplies.

Cleaning With Razor Blades

The droppings of your tokay may become stubbornly cemented to the sides of your terrarium. A handy tool for removing them is a razor blade. You can just scrape at the feces with the blade, and they should come off in a few passes. Only use the razor blade if you have a glass enclosure, though. If you are using an acrylic or PVC cage, the razor blade will scratch up the sides.

When choosing the proper place for the heat lamp, be sure to place it at one end of the cage or the other, creating a warm zone and a cooler zone. Making one side of the cage warmer than the other is very important to reptiles. Reptiles control their temperature (thermoregulation) through their behavior, moving to warmer areas when they need to warm up and moving to cooler areas when they cool down. This is called behavioral thermoregulation. If there are not two distinct temperate zones in your cage, your gecko may become stressed because it is unable to regulate its body temperature.

Thermometers
Always use a thermometer to be sure you are providing the proper temperatures. Digital ones are the most accurate. Do not use the adhesive strip thermometers, because they can be off by several degrees.

Commercially made thermostats are also commonly available today and are much less expensive than in years past. Using one of these thermostats will allow you to control your temperatures more accurately and create a much safer environment for your geckos.

Cage Maintenance

Maintenance is very important to the overall health and happiness of your pet. Part of keeping your tokay gecko happy and healthy is the maintenance of its environment.

Cleaning a Simple Setup

If using one of the more simplified caging designs, you can simply empty out the old substrate and wash the cage out with a water/bleach solution mixed at a ratio of about one part bleach to ten parts water (10 percent). Be sure to rinse the enclosure out thoroughly until there is no residual bleach left in it (you can determine if the bleach is gone by smelling the cage), and allow to

Tokay geckos are very fast and can easily get away when the lid to their cage is opened for feeding or cleaning. Always keep one eye on the geckos!

Quick & Easy Tokay Gecko Care

The business end of a tokay gecko can do a fair bit of damage. Generally though, they're all bark and little bite.

Housing Your Tokay Gecko

air dry. Soak all of the cage furniture in a bleach and water solution of similar strength as well. To be an effective disinfectant, the bleach solution must be in contact with the cage and furnishings for at least 15 minutes. Once cleaned and dry, reset the cage with your substrate, water bowl, and cage furniture. You should perform this maintenance roughly every other week, depending on the number of geckos that are housed in the enclosure and how fast the cage gets dirty.

Cleaning a Naturalistic Vivarium

If you have a naturalistic vivarium, then the cleaning process is a bit different because you cannot simply dump out the entire contents and assault the filth with a powerful bleach solution. Since live plants are nearly always used in a setup like this, you'll have to use a solution that is eco-friendly—unless you want to kill the plants.

Start by removing any decor that is not fixed to the sides or back of the vivarium, and spray down the walls of the cage with your cleaning solution—usually warm water and a sturdy scrub brush is all that's really needed. Feel free to wash the cage décor, too.

Because the live plants and soil will act as a sort of mini ecosystem, there should be no need to change the soil very frequently. The bacteria that live in the base layer will break down and destroy the waste products, so you'll probably only need to change the substrate every six months and sometimes even less. With that, let your nose be your guide, but you should still spot clean any wastes and dead feeder insects you happen to notice. Remember to always provide clean water for drinking, and wash the bowl and change the water daily. If this basic maintenance is provided, you should have few problems keeping your gecko happy and healthy.

Feeding Your Tokay Gecko

Tokay geckos will consume a large variety of foods, thus making them generally easy to feed in captivity. When tokays are babies, small insects (i.e., crickets, roaches, etc.) are their most common prey, while larger tokays have been known to consume larger insects and even small birds and mammals if the opportunity arises.

Offering a wide variety of foods is important to keeping a captive tokay gecko healthy. By offering a diverse diet, you help ensure that your tokay gecko is not lacking any essential vitamins, minerals, and amino acids. And because many types of live, dried, and frozen foods are commonly available at many pet stores, feeding your gecko should pose little difficulty. Never be afraid to offer new foods to your tokay—you'll be surprised to see what they may accept.

Crickets

The most commonly sold food for insectivorous reptiles is crickets. For many years, crickets were raised commercially on a large scale for fishing bait, but with the popularity of pet reptiles soaring over the past decade or so, cricket breeders found a new and much larger market for their product. Today, nearly every pet retailer in the United States carries crickets. Many of them even carry several other feeder insects, too, which is even more beneficial to your tokay gecko's health.

Choosing the Right-Sized Crickets

Dealers usually supply a variety of sizes to fit your needs. Baby tokay geckos will generally consume 1/2 -inch crickets, larger juveniles and subadult tokay geckos will usually consume 1-inch crickets, and adults have no problem with full-grown crickets, which may be as large as 2 inches.

Crickets are an excellent staple for a gecko's diet. Be sure to change it up here and there though—who wants to eat the same thing every day?

Quick & Easy Tokay Gecko Care

This cricket is feeding on flaked foods for tropical fishes, which is an excellent food to gut load your crickets with prior to offering them to the geckos.

Buying Crickets

Many pet retailers sell crickets by the dozen, but for a lower cost, you may want to consider purchasing the crickets in boxes of 500 to 1,000 at a time. In either case, it is best to take your crickets home and set them up. This will afford you the opportunity to "gut load" your crickets and make them a more efficient and healthy diet. This process just ensures that you aren't feeding a hollow, unfulfilling diet to your gecko.

Crickets alone do not have excellent nutritional value if they themselves have not been fed a good diet. Always buy crickets from the store before you are ready to feed your gecko, and set them up in their own cage where they can be fortified (gut loaded). Small plastic pet habitats make good cricket keepers for a large quantity (say 500 or so) of the insects. Larger plastic tubs make good cricket keepers for box lots of 500 to 1,000 crickets.

Gut Loading Your Crickets

Gut loading your crickets prior to feeding them to your tokay gecko is a great way to ensure that your lizard gets all of the essential nutrients that he'll need to stay healthy. The most important thing about gut loading is actually finding the proper

Feeding Your Tokay Gecko

diet to feed the crickets. There are many high-quality commercial cricket diets available from pet retailers. If you can't locate a commercial cricket diet, then you can also use chicken scratch, which can be found at most feed supply stores.

Crickets can be ravenous feeders, so be sure to offer them a lot of the gut-loading material. Don't be afraid to either sprinkle enough of the meal across the bottom of the holding cage for it to cover the bottom, almost like a substrate. Because the material is so dry, be sure to give the crickets water or some vegetation to hydrate them. Carrots or the stems of leafy greens seem to work well and provide additional vitamins that will be passed on to your gecko.

If providing a water dish to the crickets, make sure you put a sponge or cotton in the water so that the crickets do not get trapped in it and drown. Once the crickets have consumed the food for a day or two, they are then ready to be fed to your gecko.

When feeding your gecko, be sure to only feed as many as the gecko can eat. Never leave excess crickets in the cage, as the crickets can sometimes attack and chew on the lizard's skin and appendages. This may cause damage to the lizard, negatively affecting its health.

Various mealworms also make wonderful additions to the diet of tokay geckos.

Other Feeder Insects

Aside from crickets, there are many other types of live feeder insects that can be used for feeding your tokay gecko. For example, meal-

Wild-Collected Insects

Feeding wild-collected insects is also an option that's open to you, and it can add variety to the diets of your herps. If you have the ambition to catch wild insects, they can make a welcome snack for your geckos. Do not ever use wild insects if you have any reason to believe they have come in contact with insecticides, though, as contaminated feeders could be fatal to your pets. Large roaches, moths, and locusts are especially enjoyed by a larger gecko.

worms, locusts, roaches, earthworms, super worms, wax worms, moths, butter worms, and tomato horned worms are just a sample of what's available as alternative food sources for many types of reptiles, including your tokay gecko. When many of these insects first hit the market, they were considered treats

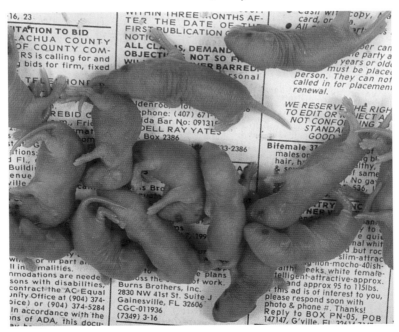

Small, live pinkie mice are welcomed treats for larger tokays.

rather than staple diets and were not as readily available as they are today.

Today, you can choose any or all of the mentioned insects to help vary the diet of your gecko. Thankfully, most of them don't present any problems if fed in moderation. Try not to feed only one type of any food; this way, you will keep the diet as varied as possible. Tokay geckos are generally receptive to many, if not all, of the aforementioned foods.

Rodents

Small mammals, like rodents, can be offered to adult tokay geckos In fact, feeding rodents gives you yet another dietary

Supplementation

When feeding any domestically raised insects to your tokay gecko, you'll need to supplement its diet with a vitamin/mineral supplement. Because most of these insects have a higher proportion of phosphorous compared to calcium, it's necessary to provide a good quality calcium supplement from time to time as well. Calcium with vitamin D_3 is available from many manufacturers, and your feeder insects should be dusted with such a powder on a regular basis. Not to mention, providing additional calcium will help to prevent any bone or growth problems.

Speaking of bone problems, although not common in tokay geckos, rare cases of metabolic bone disease have sometimes been found. Metabolic bone disease (MBD) is a calcium deficiency that reptiles in captivity sometimes develop as a result of an improper diet or the lack of full-spectrum lighting. Because full-spectrum lighting is not needed for the care of tokay geckos, providing a varied diet and using good-quality supplements from time to time is the best preventative for MBD.

option for your gecko. Large specimens will eagerly consume pinky and small fuzzy mice with ease. These small mice, which can be purchased from most pet retailers, are excellent sources of protein and calcium and can help to keep your gecko big and strong.

Tweezers can be used to feed geckos that are hidden deep in plants or other hiding places.

Just as with crickets, it's best to gut load your feeder mice with some type of high-quality feed, like those that are fed to hamsters, gerbils, or preferably, lab rodents.

As a cage litter, use aspen or other pine shavings. Always avoid using cedar shavings, as the phenols in cedar can be toxic to reptiles. You should also always provide clean drinking water for the rodents.

Feeding

In most cases, tokay geckos should be fed live prey because it's generally very difficult to get them to eat foods that are not moving given the fact that their feeding stimuli is based on movement. When feeding your geckos, always offer appropriately sized foods. A good rule of thumb is that those foods that are approximately 1/2 the size of the gecko's head will usually be consumed with little difficulty.

Because tokay geckos are nocturnal, they'll be most active and prefer to feed at night—especially when you first get them. Recently, a new type of feeding bowl has been manufactured that takes a dead food source, such as a freeze-dried cricket, and

Dirty water bowls are trouble waiting to happen. Always clean out debris as soon as you notice it accumulating in the bowl.

Quick & Easy Tokay Gecko Care

Healthy tokays should aggressively feed on a wide assortment of foods.

causes it to bounce around and appear alive through some method of vibration. This ingenious piece of equipment has been known to be effective in getting lizards that will only take live prey to actively pursue a dead or prepared food item. This bowl just gives another option for food presentation and allows an easier feed-from-a-can approach. Remember that the effectiveness may vary from animal to animal, and you may still have to feed live foods.

Water

The tokay gecko is one arboreal species that will use a water dish—unlike so many other arboreal species. Generally, arboreal lizards will not venture down to the bottom of the cage to obtain water, so for those species you should provide a water dish that is elevated off the cage's floor a bit. The tokay will actively pursue water that's been placed anywhere in the cage.

Feeding Your Tokay Gecko

Generally, arboreal animals will not venture down to the bottom of a cage to drink. However, tokay geckos are an exception and can often be seen drinking from a water bowl placed on the enclosure's floor.

The water bowl should be washed daily, and new water should be provided. Like many other species of geckos, tokays will also lap at droplets of water on the cage's décor and such when misted. In the wild, condensation that collects on trees or leaves is the primary source of water for many arboreal species—including the tokay gecko. Mist the cage lightly once or twice a day, as this will help to keep the humidity up and give the gecko another opportunity to drink.

Breeding Your Tokay Gecko

C aptive-bred reptiles of all types are much more frequently offered for sale than in the past, and tokay geckos are no exception. Tokay geckos have generally been a relatively inexpensive lizard because they were always collected from the wild, but now they're being bred in captivity and in some cases offered for sale as well-started (already eating and in good health) and sometimes even tame juveniles. The best part is that their prices haven't gone up, either, unlike some other types of captive-bred reptiles, where captive-bred specimens can be several times the cost of their wild-collected counterparts.

Due to their large size and colorful bodies, these lizards have become increasingly popular now that people see how they can be somewhat social pets. A few genetic abnormalities have arisen from captive breeding that has also sparked a renewed buzz about these geckos. Calico, leucistic, and albino traits have all come forth in the past few years, and these new color morphs give people the chance to care for something that is a bit different than the run-of-the-mill wild-type color scheme.

Sexing

Once they reach sexual maturity, tokay geckos are very easy to sex. Large angular rows of pre-anal or femoral pores are present on males and absent in females. Males will also have enlarged hemipenal bulges at the base of their tails. Males can also be identified by their loud vocalization that is used in courtship to attract the female gecko. In many cases, the males are also larger in size than females, but this is not an accurate method of sex determination since age would come into play here and unless you've raised your geckos from a hatchling, it's very difficult to tell their age.

Male tokays are generally larger than females, and they also tend to make louder vocalizations, too.

Quick & Easy Tokay Gecko Care

Some Quick & Easy Tips to Breeding Success

1. During winter months, keep the photoperiod (amount of daily light) to a minimum.

2. Maintain light similar to your normal daylight hours (~8-9 hours per day).

3. Feed your geckos a more basic diet, but don't jeopardize the animal's normal body weight by feeding them too little; just feed a bit less variety.

4. If you are misting your cage regularly, cut back to once a day or once every other day to lower the humidity during these months.

5. Come spring, you'll need to increase the humidity by misting more frequently, as well as adjusting the photoperiod by increasing the time that the lights remain on.

6. Next, begin to provide a very full and varied diet again, just as your tokay geckos were being fed before the winter set in. After several weeks, mating should occur.

Luckily, tokay geckos don't require very specialized preparation for mating.

Taking the Right Steps

First and foremost, when breeding any types of reptiles, you will need to make sure you have at least one healthy, mature male and female.. Having a group of one male to several females will make a nice small colony. Some geckos that are bred in captivity need very special and specific conditioning to get them to breed, but thankfully, this is not the case with the tokay gecko. Some geckos need to be cycled, or put through a simulated seasonal change, to encourage them to breed. However, tokay geckos don't need this type of cooling, although there are some methods that can be used to encourage a high egg yield.

During mating, the male and female will likely dance back and forth on the side of the cage. When copulation occurs, the male gecko will grab the female by the neck. Breeding females will usually have visible neck scars as a result of the males grasping onto them.

Preparing for Egg laying

Once copulation occurs, you will need to prepare for egg laying.

Small dishes of calcium should be provided during the breeding season so the female can lick up the powder—this will ensure that she has enough calcium for successful egg laying.

Providing a place for the female tokay to lay her eggs is not as easy as for some other geckos, such as leopard or fat-tailed geckos. Tokay geckos are egg gluers, and they stick their eggs to many different surfaces. They lay two hard-shelled eggs once or twice a month for about five months. The female uses her hind legs to move the eggs into what she considers a suitable place. She can stick them to the glass, water bowl, or cage furniture. Once stuck to these surfaces, the eggs are nearly impossible to remove without breaking.

Incubators

Commercial incubators can be purchased on the Internet or in some retail pet shops. An incubator can also be built out of a Styrofoam cooler or simple fish aquarium. If using a Styrofoam cooler, simply purchase a submersible aquarium heater and some ceiling egg crates. Cut the egg crate to size and wedge it into the cooler so that it is at least 6 inches from the bottom. This will provide you a platform on which to put your containers with your eggs.

Next, fill the bottom of the cooler with water and add the water heater. Set the heater and use a thermometer to make sure you maintain the proper temperatures for incubation. Cut some small holes in the sides of the cooler for air exchange, and you have a homemade incubator. This can also be achieved in the same fashion using an aquarium, but you will need to get something to sit in the bottom of the tank to rest the egg crate on. You will also need to cut a Styrofoam lid to cover the tank and keep in the humidity. If using the Styrofoam cooler technique, always be sure to check and make sure there is water in the cooler to avoid a fire.

Leaving the Eggs With the Adults

If your female tokay gecko has laid her eggs in a place from which you simply cannot remove them—like deep within the plantings of a naturalistic vivarium—then you can attempt to incubate them in their cage. If this is the case, try to maintain temperatures of 80° to 86°F during the time the eggs are in the cage, and keep the relative humidity at about 75 percent or so.

Many times, success with leaving the eggs with the adults comes in a naturalistic vivarium, where the incubation time for the eggs is the same as with an artificial setting and can take anywhere from 65 to 200 days. If you are fortunate enough to have these eggs hatch in the enclosure, you can safely maintain and rear the babies with the parents. Disturbed hatchlings in these environments have actually been observed seeking protection from the parent geckos. However, if adequate diets are provided, baby tokay geckos can be reared to adulthood within the same enclosure as the parents. If the baby geckos are removed from the environment for more than a day, do not try to reintroduce them, because they will most likely be eaten.

Incubating the Eggs

Once your gecko has laid eggs, you'll need to incubate them. If the eggs are laid on the bottom of the cage and can be removed easily from the tank, then simply remove them without turning them at all. Tokay gecko eggs can be successfully incubated in a 1:1 ratio of vermiculite to water. You can make this mixture in a small deli cup with holes or a larger plastic shoe box with small holes drilled in it for ventilation. Place this container into your incubator.

If you are fortunate enough to have loose, single eggs, push your finger into the vermiculite mixture to make a small dent or hole about half the depth of the egg, and place each one in its own separate hole. For eggs that are glued to something such as a branch,

After an incubation period lasting between 65-200 days, baby tokays will begin hatching out of their eggs.

remove them by breaking or cutting off the piece of wood with the eggs attached, and place them into the same type of setup without turning or disturbing them.

Tokay gecko eggs should be incubated at temperatures of 80° to 86°F. These eggs generally take 65 to 200 days to hatch. Lower temperatures generally take longer to hatch. Tokays are temperature sex determined, which means you can control the gender of the offspring by the incubation temperatures. As in leopard and fat tail geckos, eggs incubated at lower temperatures yield females, and

Captive Breeding

Captive breeding is very important in the success of many species of herps and although these geckos are still imported in large numbers, this certainly may not go on forever.

Young tokays are shy and will spend much of their time hidden among root tangles, rocks, or other décor in their terrariums.

higher temperatures yield males. Temperatures of 82° to 84°F tend to give you a mix of both males and females.

Caring for Baby Tokay Geckos

Baby tokay geckos can be raised in the same basic types of caging and under the same basic conditions as adults. Be sure to keep babies in cages with smaller openings, though, because baby tokay geckos can work their way out of many nooks and crannies. Other than this, the babies really have no special specific requirements.

As with all baby reptile hatchlings, baby tokay geckos have more of a need for calcium than adults for their growing bones. Calcium supplementation should be provided every feeding for the first year or so of the gecko's life. Hatchlings also can use a bit more humidity. This helps their skin and feet to shed more easily.

Raising baby tokays can be fun and educational. Getting them used to human interaction at a young age is very helpful in making them tame and handleable. Hopefully, you will be well on your way to breeding and keeping many more generations of tokay geckos. Maybe you will be one of the lucky ones to hatch an oddity like an albino!

Health Care

Tokay geckos generally do not have a great deal of health problems. Purchasing captive-bred specimens or animals that you know have been previously treated and are established in captivity will reduce your risk of dealing with a sick animal. Once again, be sure to initially select a specimen that is as healthy as possible using the guidelines discussed earlier. However, even being very careful or purchasing captive-bred animals is not a completely foolproof way to prevent disease.

Quarantining New Animals

One of the most important things to do if you keep multiple reptiles is to quarantine any new specimens that are obtained.

Newly acquired tokays should always go through a period of quarantine.

This is the best way to prevent the animals you already have from becoming sick from a potentially infected new arrival. Always keep new animals separate from your existing ones and preferably in a separate room if possible.

A quarantine period should last for at least a week, but longer periods, such as a month or two, are much more effective and give you a more complete picture of your lizards' overall health. When caring for the quarantined animals, *always* be sure to wash your hands each time you interact with them. Whether it's changing the water, cleaning the cage, or handling them, *always* wash your hands before and after contact with the animals.

Keep a close eye on your animals during this period. Notice feeding habits, and examine the stool to make sure everything seems normal. Once you see that the animal is doing well and you and your veterinarian feel comfortable with its overall health, you should then allow it to be housed in close proximity to your other animals. The quarantine of new specimens is one of the more important aspects of successful pet ownership, so be sure to keep a close eye on them during this time.

Internal Parasites

Internal parasites can be an issue with even the healthiest animal. If observed early, they are sometimes easy to treat and eradicate. Because identifying and treating these parasites can be complex, it is best to take the animal to a veterinarian who specializes in reptiles. If you notice your gecko is rapidly loosing weight and has very loose or discolored stools, he may have some sort of internal parasite. Reptile vets can then take a stool sample and examine it under a microscope to determine how this lizard should be treated. The dosages and weights of certain medications can be critical, so it is always best to leave it up to the vet to decide the treatment.

Mites

Because many tokay geckos are still wild caught, you should inspect the lizards closely for external parasites before bringing them home from the pet shop. Sometimes small red mites can blend in with the red spots of the tokay geckos and make the mites hard to see. There are several commercial mite remedies available through your pet retailer, and all seem to work well for such infestations.

If you notice mites on your gecko, you should remove everything from the cage and clean it thoroughly with bleach. After cleaning it, be sure to rinse it thoroughly and allow it to completely dry. Keep the cage decorated as simply as possible during this treatment period. A bare bones-type setup with just a water bowl and newspaper for substrate should be used until the problem is solved. Once you are sure the mites have been eliminated, reset your cage back to normal with the proper bedding and cage furniture.

Health Care

Egg Binding

A problem that sometimes affects female geckos is something called egg binding. Egg binding is usually a direct result of improper husbandry. Either the animals were not fed a proper diet and cannot properly form eggs, or the cage is not set up for suitable egg laying. If the

Misting the gecko's cage on a regular basis will not only allow the animal to drink but will also assist in skin shedding.

lizard becomes egg bound and cannot pass the eggs, then this life-threatening issue may need veterinary attention. If you catch this quickly enough, however, a vet may be able to save your gecko's life.

Shedding

Sometimes tokay geckos will have problems with the shedding of their skin. If you notice your gecko is having a difficult time shedding, then check the humidity level in the cage, as it may be too low. Misting the gecko's cage more regularly should also help it to shed its skin a bit easier. In many instances, tokay geckos shed in pieces, so only be concerned if they seem to be having problems with the skin not coming off their feet, limbs, or eyes. If the gecko looks uncomfortable trying to get unwanted skin off, it probably is. Only at this time is it a good idea to manually help the gecko shed its skin.

Respiratory Infections

One other problem that tokay geckos occasionally experience is respiratory illness. If you notice your lizard wheezing or experiencing abnormal discharge from the nostrils, then you should be concerned. Maintaining temperatures in the low- to mid-90s will usually help to eliminate slight respiratory infections. If the problem persists and the gecko seems worse, then you should consult your vet right away. An antibiotic may be needed in extreme cases.

Other Gecko Species

I n addition to the tokay gecko, there are many other gecko species that are available from your local reptile dealer or through Internet dealers. These geckos all have very similar care and husbandry requirements as the tokay, and they are usually recommended for beginners.

Skunk or White Line Geckos

Another large gecko, which happens to be closely related to the tokay gecko, is the skunk or white line gecko. Just as with the tokay gecko, this species is also commonly imported from Indonesia. They can be very beautiful when fully acclimated, with their reddish-brown to tan color and white line that runs from the

Skunk geckos are commonly imported from Indonesia—just like tokay geckos.

base of the tail to the back of the head, where it then splits into a "y" shape and ends up over the eyes of the lizard. The tail can be white banded, but it's mostly just brown with a hint of white or with white blotches that reach to the tip.

These geckos are a bit more slender than the tokay gecko, but they can be cared for in the exact same manner. White line geckos are also being bred in small numbers in captivity, which means that some captive-bred specimens are available from time to time. Just as with tokays, they can be kept in groups of one male to several females. These geckos are egg gluers, and the eggs should be treated the same as you would with tokay geckos. Incubation takes place over 70 to 80 days.

The Gold Gecko

Gold geckos were originally imported into the United States in the early 1990s. Somewhat calmer in disposition than their close relatives, the tokays, gold geckos have become very popular and are

Gold geckos are generally calmer and less aggressive compared to tokay geckos.

Other Gecko Species

now commonly available from many pet retailers. They tolerate handling a bit more than tokay geckos or white line geckos do and can become fairly tame over a short time. Gold geckos are mostly imported from Vietnam and have fairly good survival rates.

Gold geckos are more slender compared to similar species, and they have larger eyes and a velvety skin tone. Their color is generally a golden green, with a brighter golden yellow rectangle or group of bars on the back, although their markings are highly variable overall. Because so many of these animals are imported at one time, it is possible for their condition to be poor upon arrival into the United States; this is why it's important to look over each gecko closely if you are going to buy. These geckos are not being captive bred in any numbers, but given the possibilities of captive reproduction within this genus, it is probably not far off. Care, maintenance, and breeding are similar to the tokay gecko.

Green-eyed Geckos

Green-eyed geckos are some of the larger members of their group. Much like their cousin, the tokay, green-eyed geckos have large,

Green-eyed geckos are unique in that their eyes are an emerald green in color. They are large and males may attain sizes of nearly 10 inches (25 cm) in length.

Note the white banding on the tail of this juvenile green-eyed gecko—a trait that many tokay-type species exhibit.

heavy bodies with offset heads, wide toe pads, and large eyes. They are mainly found in Burma and Thailand but can be found in other parts of southeast Asia.

Adult males can reach lengths in excess of 10 inches (25 cm), with females being slightly smaller, and females also have white rows of spots across a greenish brown background color. Green-eyed geckos lack any red coloration, which sets them apart in appearance from the tokay gecko. Most of the imports from Indonesia are probably "true" green-eyed geckos (*Gekko smithi*).

Green-eyed geckos have 8 to 14 rows of large tubercular scales around the middle of their back. Other specimens that are brought in from Thailand are most likely the more recently described *Gekko taylori*, which tend to be a bit smaller and have 16 to 19 rows of tubercles. These geckos are often a darker green or dark brown-colored geckos.

Other Gecko Species

Large gold geckos have a more velvety skin tone and tolerate handling better compared to tokays.

Quick & Easy Tokay Gecko Care

Care and maintenance of both species should be the same as it is for tokay geckos. Well-conditioned green-eyed geckos can be impressive specimens if you can find them available for sale. These geckos seem to be imported much less than tokay geckos and not as easy to come by. Again, most specimens are wild collected, but because they are not imported in such large numbers, their price is usually a bit higher.

Monarch or Butterfly Gecko

This gecko is probably not a common species that you'll see offered for sale in pet stores, and they're probably best reserved for gecko enthusiasts and rare reptile hobbyists. This species is a bit smaller than the green-eyed gecko, but it still reaches lengths of about 8 inches.

Monarch or butterfly geckos are indigenous to southern Thailand, Malaysia, and the Philippines. They are generally brownish to greenish in color, with the same basic body shape as the tokay gecko. Mainly arboreal, monarch or butterfly geckos spend much of their time in trees but have been found on the sides of houses, much like the tokay gecko.

These geckos have a very distinct pattern down their backs characterized by about ten pairs of black spots on each side. These spots are separated by a cream to white-colored stripe, which gives their pattern the illusion of a butterfly's spread wings. This type of appearance is the reason for its name. The black spots continue down the back and form into black rings around the tail, giving this species a very interesting pattern. Care and maintenance should be as the same as it would be for a tokay gecko. Breeding and egg incubation are also the same, with baby geckos emerging from their eggs after about 80 to 100 days.

CONVERSION CHART

US UNITS	MULTIPLIED BY	EQUALS METRIC UNITS
Length		
Inches	2.5400	Centimeters
Feet	0.3048	Meters
Yards	0.9144	Meters
Miles	1.6093	Kilometers
Area		
Square inches	6.4516	Square centimeters
Square feet	0.0929	Square meters
Square yards	0.8361	Square meters
Acres	0.4047	Hectares
Volume		
Cubic feet	0.0283	Cubic meters
Cubic yards	0.7646	Cubic meters
Gallons	3.7854	Liters
Weight		
Foot-pounds	1.3830	Newton-meters
Pounds	0.4536	Kilograms

Temperature

Fahrenheit to Celsius: Subtract 32 from the Fahrenheit temperature. Divide the answer by 9, then multiply by 5.

Quick & Easy Tokay Gecko Care

Resources

CLUBS & SOCIETIES

Amphibian, Reptile & Insect Association
Liz Price
23 Windmill Rd
Irthlingsborough
Wellingborough NN9 5RJ
England

American Society of Ichthyologists and Herpetologists
Maureen Donnelly, Secretary
Grice Marine Laboratory
Florida International University
Biological Sciences
11200 SW 8th St.
Miami, FL 33199
Telephone: (305) 348-1235
E-mail: asih@fiu.edu
www.asih.org

The Global Gecko Association
c/o Leann Christenson
1155 Cameron Cove Circle
Leeds, Alabama 35094
E-mail: membership@gekkota.com
http://www.gekkota.com/

Society for the Study of Amphibians and Reptiles (SSAR)
Marion Preest, Secretary
The Claremont Colleges
925 N. Mills Ave.
Claremont, CA 91711
Telephone: 909-607-8014
E-mail: mpreest@jsd.claremont.edu
www.ssarherps.org

VETERINARY RESOURCES

Association of Reptile and Amphibian Veterinarians
P.O. Box 605
Chester Heights, PA 19017

Phone: 610-358-9530
Fax: 610-892-4813
E-mail: ARAVETS@aol.com
www.arav.org

RESCUE AND ADOPTION SERVICES

ASPCA
424 East 92nd Street
New York, NY 10128-6801
Phone: (212) 876-7700
E-mail: information@aspca.org
www.aspca.org

RSPCA (UK)
Wilberforce Way
Southwater
Horsham, West Sussex RH13 9RS
Telephone: 0870 3335 999
www.rspca.org.uk

WEB SITES

Rhacodactylus ciliatus
http://www.rhacodactylus.net

The Reptile Rooms
http://www.reptilerooms.org/

Gecko Network
http://www.leopardgecko.co.uk/

MAGAZINES

Herp Digest
www.herpdigest.org

Reptiles Magazine
P.O. Box 6050
Mission Viejo, CA 92690
www.animalnetwork.com/reptiles

Index

Photo Credits

M. Bacon, 7, 12, 55
R. Bartlett, 8, 49, 58-59
A. Both, 28(t), 54, 57
I. Francais, 14, 19, 22, 42
J. Gerholdt, 52
M. Gilroy, 10
W.R. Marra, 1, 46

G & C Merker, 6, 17, 56
A. Norman, 33, 44
M. Smith, 16
K. Switak, 3-4, 60
T.F.H. Photo Archives, 5, 11, 13, 18, 21, 23-26, 28(b), 30-31, 34-37, 39-41, 43, 50-51